abc menagerie

Sculptures by Elena V. Targioni · Written by M.H. Clark · Designed by Heidi Rodriguez

This book's filled...

with creatures you might think you've met,
but I promise you'll find them brand new.
They live in a world of wild alphabets,
so you cannot find them in the zoo.

Some are furry, or spotted, or covered in feathers,
or silly, as you will soon see.
They love to read books and they love to learn letters,
exactly like you and like me!

So, shall we get started on what we've begun?
We'll travel from A on to Z,
and then by the end, when you've met everyone,
you'll know the whole menagerie!

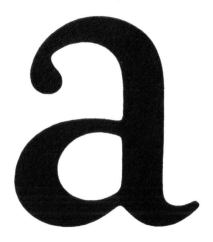

AH-yo

AYO THE AARDVARK

Ayo loves keys, and collects them galore.

They jingle wherever she goes.

She has keys to the attics and keys to the doors

of every termite she knows.

broon-HILL-deh

 BRUNHILDE THE BEAR

Brunhilde dips into the cold-running river,

the fish swim right up to her eyes.

But the thought of eating them sets her aquiver;

for lunch, she has blackberry pie.

kee-OH-nee

CHIONE THE CAMEL

Chione lives out in the hot desert sun
but has such a passion for flowers
she carries some with her wherever she runs
and waters them twice every hour.

duh-GAH

DEGAS THE DOG

Degas makes his drawings in all shades of blue
with pencils he stores 'round his collar.
He draws beautiful landscapes and fine portraits too,
as his pencils grow smaller and smaller.

EH-shay

ESHE THE ELEPHANT

Eshe's nose is a cappuccinose;

it's perfect for balancing cups.

How convenient to know that wherever she goes,

she has something to hold her mug up.

frits

FRITZ THE FOX

Fritz keeps his sharp-smelling nose in the air
as he watches the birds in their flight.
They travel so far, just as high as they dare,
while Fritz wishes he were a kite.

gah-LEE-nah

GALINA THE GOAT

Galina starts tending her garden in spring

when the air smells sweetly of clover.

She grows garlic and beans and cooks everything

at a party when summer is over.

* awn-REE *

HENRI THE HARE

Henri's alarm goes off early each day.

He packs a small salad or two,

then he ties his ears up, so they're out of his way,

and hops off as soon as he's through.

* igg-NAY-she-us *

⤳ IGNACIUS THE IGUANA ↫

Ignacius sends frequent letters to friends

who live in faraway lands.

He writes in blue ink with the ten fountain pens

that he always keeps close at hand.

yeh-SEHN-ee-uh

JESENIA THE JAGUAR

Jesenia's spots just want to escape;

they're bouncy as new rubber balls.

She's tried sticking them on with plenty of tape,

but they simply won't listen at all!

KAI-ee-mah

Kyeema the Kangaroo

Kyeema's Australia's busiest mother.

Her groceries fit in her pouch.

And when she gets home from one errand or other,

she just wants to rest on the couch.

1

loo-see-AHN-ah

LUCIANA THE LLAMA

Luciana, when spitting, has excellent aim;

there's no one she couldn't surpass.

She especially loves to launch paper planes,

but her teacher forbids it in class.

MURR-ee

❧ Murray the Mole ❧

Murray goes tunneling deep underground—

it's dark wherever you look.

He carries three lights so that when he sits down,

he can read his library books.

NEE-gahk

NIGAQ THE NARWHAL

Nigaq, you'll notice, is long in the nose;

the rest of his family is too.

But he can catch all of the donuts you'll throw

without even having to chew.

oh-FEEL-yah

OPHELIA THE OPOSSUM

Ophelia's three children love games in the park;

they snack and they swing and they slide.

She takes them each evening, as soon as it's dark,

then carries them home, sleepy-eyed.

PER-siv-al

Percival the Pig

Percival's dinners are rich and gourmet,

with plenty of chocolate éclairs.

Whenever he's had one too many that day,

his safety valves let out the air.

KWIN-tess-uh

❧ Quintessa the Quail ❧

Quintessa tilts backwards to take in the sun;

its light tastes like lemons in spring.

The rays hit her feathers and warm every one,

from her tail to the tips of her wings.

roo-NAH-koh

RUNAKO THE RHINO

Runako's a giant, but loves gentle things,
like fluttering bright butterflies.
They visit for tea and their soft-beating wings
bring tears of joy to his eyes.

S

SHELL-done

SHELDON THE SHEEP

Sheldon once lay wide awake in his bed

all night, tangled up in the sheets.

But now he just counts numbers up in his head

and finds he can fall right to sleep!

twee

❧ Thuy the Turtle ❧

Thuy is a traveler extraordinaire;
she knows all the major routes well.
If her favorite motels have no room to spare,
there's a pillow tucked into her shell.

UL-tih-muh

ULTIMA THE UMBRELLABIRD

Ultima's egg is beginning to hatch
in the shade of her pink parasol.
She hears the youngbrellabird starting to scratch
and sings to it with her sweet call.

VICK-rum

Vikram the Vulture

Vikram wins medals all over the world
for daring and great feats of flight.
His fans gasp at all of his beautiful twirls
and clap their hands loud in delight.

WAY-vah

WAVA THE WALRUS

Wava ties two bright balloons to her tail;
they make her feel airy and free.
She's planning some day for a ten-balloon sail
that will take her right over the sea.

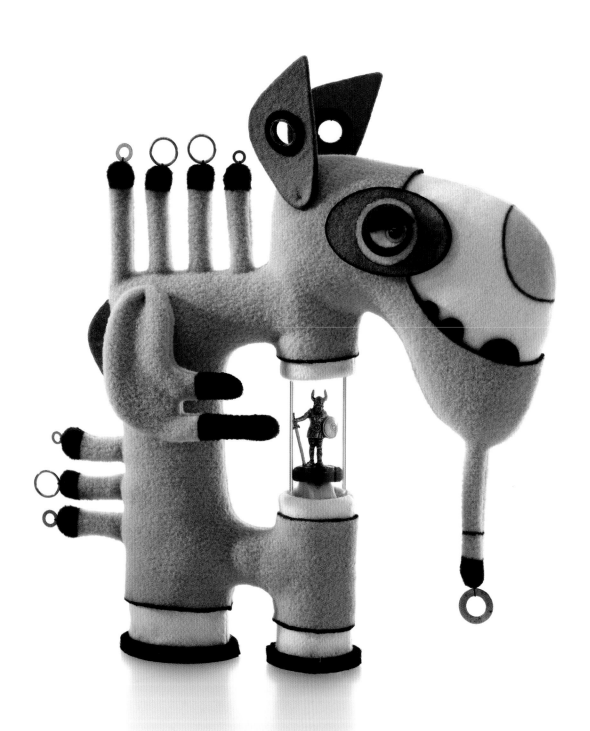

ZAYV-ee-er

❧ XAVIER THE X-IMAL ❧

Xavier loves to eat all kinds of toys—
he's always hungry for more.
His very best friends are the girls and the boys
who leave their playthings on the floor.

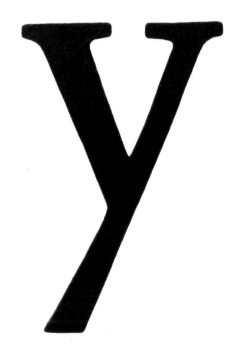

YOU-ree

YURI THE YAK

Yuri breathes quiet and clear mountain air;

he takes a rest under the trees.

The world feels so peaceful whenever he's there,

and his back gets embellished with leaves.

zah-REB

Zareb the Zebra

Zareb was born bare, without any stripes,
and knew that he wanted some help.
His tailor was able to make it all right
with nine simply beautiful belts.

AARDVARKS live in the grasslands and woodlands of central and southern Africa. Aardvarks sleep during the day and wake at night, when they hunt for ants and termites with their extra-long and sticky tongues. Their strong feet and thick claws are ideal for digging into the hard mounds where termites live.

From the polar bear of the Arctic to the Kodiak bear of Alaska and the giant panda of China, bears of different kinds live all over the world. **BEARS** are excellent climbers and swimmers. Their curious nature and good sense of smell help them to find the plants and animals they eat.

CAMELS live in the dry deserts and plains of Asia and Africa. Their humps help to store energy for long trips or for when food is scarce. Dromedary (or Arabian) camels have one hump on their backs while Bactrian camels have two! All camels are well adapted to heat and are capable of surviving long periods of drought, when water is scarce.

The **DOGS** that you see in your neighborhood every day are relatives of the wild wolves, foxes, and jackals of the world. Dogs were domesticated, or tamed, by people thousands of years ago because they were so useful and made good companions. Today, there are hundreds of different dog breeds in the world, many bred for specific jobs and looks.

ELEPHANTS are the largest land animals. At birth, a baby elephant can weigh around 200 pounds! There are two types of elephant: African and Asian. Both species of African elephants, forest and bush elephants, are larger than Asian elephants. Elephants are herbivores (plant eaters) and use their trunks to smell, eat, wash, and communicate.

FOXES of different kinds live in many climates, from dry deserts to the snowy Arctic. Foxes look different depending on where they live, with coats in colors that help them blend in with their surroundings. They have a distinctive pounce when they catch small animals and insects, but they may also eat berries, eggs, and some plants.

Wild **GOATS** live all over the world, from Europe to the Middle East and Asia. Goats were domesticated around 10,000 years ago and are bred today for milk and meat. Goats are excellent climbers and very curious; they like to explore their world and nibble on all kinds of things, though they mostly eat grasses and plants.

HARES are close relatives of rabbits, but they are generally larger and have longer ears. The hare's strong hind legs help it reach speeds of up to 45 miles per hour! Hares eat plants, grasses, and bark; sleep in nests they build on the ground; and tend to be very shy creatures.

IGUANAS are lizards found all over the world in a variety of climates. Some iguanas live near water and are excellent swimmers, while others live in tropical and subtropical forests and are good tree climbers. Iguanas that live in deserts have adapted to live in dry climates. Most iguanas eat fruits, flowers, and leaves, with an occasional bug or two.

JAGUARS are big cats and live in North America and Central and South America. Jaguars are predators, hunting for many different kinds of animals with quick paws and a very strong jaw. Jaguars hunt alone and prefer to live in dense forests where there is water for swimming.

KANGAROOS live in Australia and Papua New Guinea. They are part of a group called marsupials—animals who keep their young babies in pocket-like pouches until the babies are old enough to leave. Kangaroos are the only large mammals that move by hopping; their strong back legs help them get around quickly to escape predators and to find food.

LLAMAS live in the hills and mountains of South America, where they eat plants and grasses. Llamas love the company of other llamas, and they live in groups called herds. Their long, wooly coats that keep them warm during the cold evenings can be sheared and used for weaving into clothing and blankets.

MOLES are excellent at digging and burrowing. Wherever they are found, from North America to Europe and Asia, moles tunnel underground, where they find earthworms and insects to eat. The eyes of a mole can tell daylight from darkness but cannot otherwise see at all; moles feel their way around with their whiskers and sensitive noses.

NARWHALS live in the chilly waters of the Arctic, where they eat fish, shrimp, and squid and stay warm with a thick layer of fat called blubber. Narwhals have a single tusk, which can grow up to ten feet long and is filled with nerves that help the narwhal to know more about the temperature, pressure, and saltiness of the water around it.

OPOSSUMS, like kangaroos and other marsupials, keep their babies in a pouch until they are old enough to care for themselves. Opossums are nocturnal—awake at night and asleep during the day. They will eat many different kinds of meals, from small animals and birds to fruits and plants and garbage from backyard trash cans.

The **PIGS** that you see on a farm are domesticated, or tamed, versions of wild pigs called boars, which are native to many different parts of the world. Pigs are omnivores, eating a wide variety of plants and animals for food. They use their sensitive snouts to sniff out a meal and to dig in the ground to find it.

QUAILS live in forests, fields, and grasslands in many parts of the world, building their nests on the ground. They eat seeds and small insects. Most quails cannot fly for long trips, because their wings are so short. They travel by flying in quick spurts and by running very quickly along the ground.

RHINOCEROS are herbivores that live in Africa and southern Asia. Rhinos have such poor eyesight that they sometimes charge (run at) trees and rocks, mistaking them for something threatening. Some species of rhinoceros have one horn, while others have two, but all rhino horns are made out of keratin—the same material as your fingernails.

SHEEP were one of the first animals to be domesticated by early humans because their wool, milk, and meat were so useful. Sheep are often raised in large groups called flocks, which move from place to place as they graze on grasses and other plants. Sheep have a strong instinct to follow a leader and respond to herding by dogs and humans.

TURTLES are reptiles that live in a wide range of habitats all over the world. Some live on land, some in fresh water, and others in oceans. All turtles have a shell with an upper part (the carapace) and a lower part (the plastron). The whole shell is attached to the turtle, acting as a form of protection, like a shield.

UMBRELLABIRDS live in Central and South American rainforests. Their name comes from a bunch of black feathers that droop forward from the top of the head and look a little like a small umbrella. Umbrellabirds have a wattle on their neck that inflates like a balloon and helps to make their loud calls even louder!

VULTURES are birds that scavenge, which means they eat sick, dead, and decaying animals. Vultures live in almost all parts of the world and are a very valuable part of the food chain because they help to clean up carcasses. They have extra-strong stomachs and digestive systems and are able to eat things that would make most other animals sick.

WALRUSES live in the cold waters of the Arctic seas, where they find shellfish, crabs, and other seafood with their sensitive whiskers. Walruses can weigh up to 1.5 tons and stay warm with a layer of blubber. Walruses use their tusks to break holes in thick ice and to help them out of the water onto ice platforms and beaches, where they love to socialize.

X-IMALS live all over the world, particularly in houses and schools where they forage under beds, couches, and tables for toys children may have dropped. Though they are friendly, they are quite shy and try very hard not to be seen by humans. Messy rooms are their ideal habitat since they can find plenty of food without being spotted.

YAKS are long-haired members of the cow family found in mountainous areas of central Asia. Yaks are perfectly suited to the cold mountain areas where they live, with large lungs that help them get oxygen from the air and long coats to keep them warm. They travel far in search of the mosses, grasses, and lichens that they eat.

ZEBRAS are wild members of the horse family, with stripes in shades of black, white, and gray. Each zebra has its own completely unique pattern of stripes. These stripes help to camouflage, or hide, the zebra from predators like lions, which are color blind. The stripes look very much like the lines and shadows of the grasses where zebras live.

FIN

ELENA V. TARGIONI | ARTIST

was born in Prato in 1970. In 1999, she graduated from the sculpture program at the Academy of Fine Arts in Florence. She has worked with fabric since 2000 and currently operates a studio with a friend in the heart of Florence.

Three main ingredients always accompany Elena's work: amazement, tenderness, and humor. These elements have found their way into each of the animals in this book, along with a special smile—the smile that comes with the excitement of the creative process.

Elena hopes to give 26 smiles to each young reader.

"dedicato ai miei genitori e a Matilde"

M.H. CLARK | WRITER

is a Rhode Island native, and so, comes mostly from the ocean. After years of living in cities far and wide she now lives on the West Coast, where she is a poet, writer, bookbinder, and proprietor of Seattle's Poem Store.

WITH SPECIAL THANKS TO THE ENTIRE COMPENDIUM FAMILY.

SCULPTURES BY: *Elena V. Targioni*

WRITTEN BY: *M.H. Clark*

DESIGNED BY: *Heidi Rodriguez*

EDITED BY: *Jennifer Pletsch*

CREATIVE DIRECTION BY: *Sarah Forster*

Library of Congress Control Number: 2011933975

ISBN: 978-1-932319-54-5

1st printing. Printed in China with soy inks.

57605